XTREME ART

DRAW MANGA VILLAINS!

CHRISTOPHER HART

WATSON-GUPTILL PUBLICATIONS/NEW YORK

INTRODUCTION

Bad guys and gals are so much fun to draw! They can be powerful, greedy, sneaky, and ruthless. They have the coolest powers and the flashiest costumes.

Some of today's most popular villains can be found in manga. *Manga* is the Japanese word for "comics." Manga characters are noted for their big, shiny eyes, tiny noses, and far-out hairstyles. Now you can draw in this famous style, too!

This book will help you draw all kinds of evil manga villains quickly and easily. Each drawing is broken down into four simple steps. Start by tracing or drawing step 1. Then add the red lines in steps 2, 3, and 4. It's that easy!

You'll find all kinds of villains to draw, starting with easier ones and getting a little harder as you go. A few of the drawings have backgrounds, which you can either trace or draw if you like.

So are you ready to draw sinister robots, evil mutants, devilish witches, and fierce fighters? All you need is a pencil, paper, and your imagination!

Tips for Using This Book

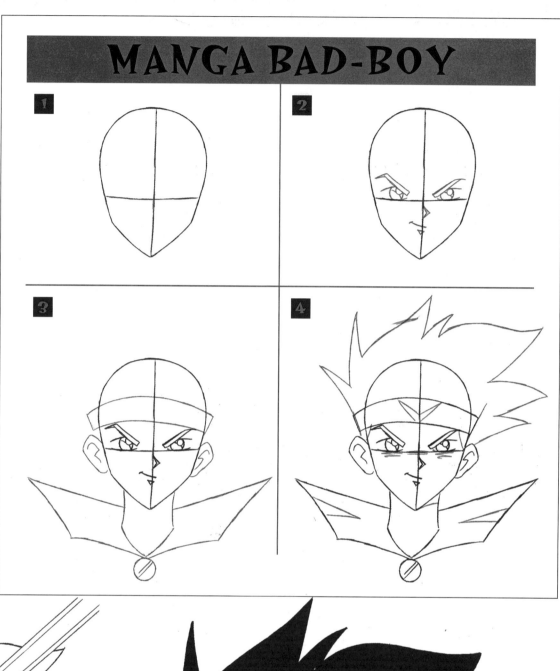

MANGA BAD-BOY

Trace or draw what you see in step 1. Then add the new lines (shown in red) in steps 2, 3, and 4. Draw with a light, sketchy line. Don't worry about getting it perfect on the first try.

When you've finished the steps, erase the guidelines (the criss-crosses) and any other lines you don't want to keep. Go over the other lines to make them darker.

Color it in, and you've got a clean, bold drawing!

THE BASICS

Let's start with some basics for drawing manga villains.

Manga characters are famous for their big eyes. But the eyes of evil characters are drawn differently from the eyes of good characters.

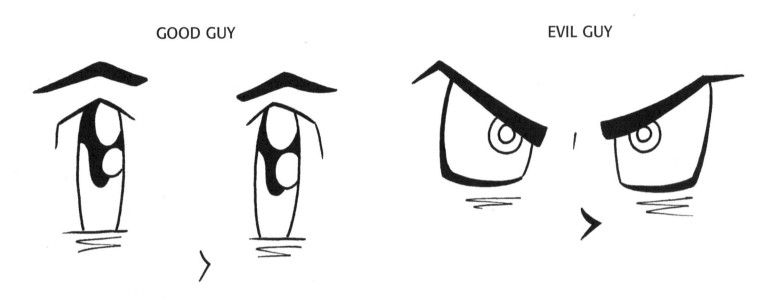

GOOD GUY

EVIL GUY

Good guys have eyes that are very tall. Their pupils are big, with giant shines.

Bad guys have small, beady eyes. Their eyebrows go down. The lines under their eyes are thick and dark.

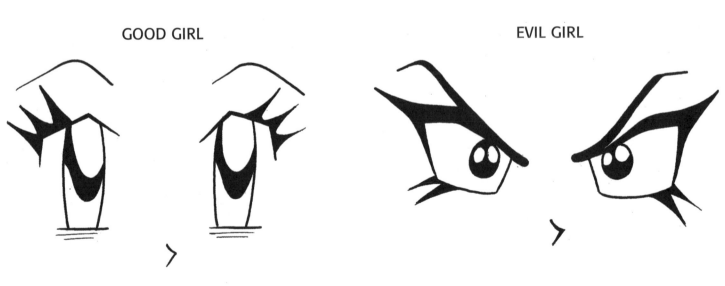

GOOD GIRL

EVIL GIRL

Good girls have eyes that are wide open, with big shines. They have thin eyebrows and eyelashes on top.

Bad girls have smaller eyes, with thick eyelashes on top, and even some on the bottom. They have thicker eyebrows that slant down.

Bad guys and gals are really just good guys and gals with a few simple but important changes.

Here's a basic good guy. He's got a pleasant, simple face.

Give him thick eyebrows that go down, and darken his eyeballs. Add a smile. (Angry eyes combined with a smile make a character look evil.) Now give him spiked hair.

Add an eye patch, an ear set, and a big collar. Give him a second patch of spiked hair in front. Instant bad guy!

Good girls are cute and simple. Evil girls are fancy, glamorous, and wear lots of makeup.

GOOD GIRL

Thin eyelashes

No eyelashes on bottom (or very tiny ones)

Neat hairstyle, like pigtails

Simple earrings

EVIL GIRL

Eyebrows slant down

Spiked or uneven hairstyle

Very thick and pointy upper eyelashes

Thick eyelashes on the bottom, too

Evil-looking jewelry (often in the shape of animals or creepy things)

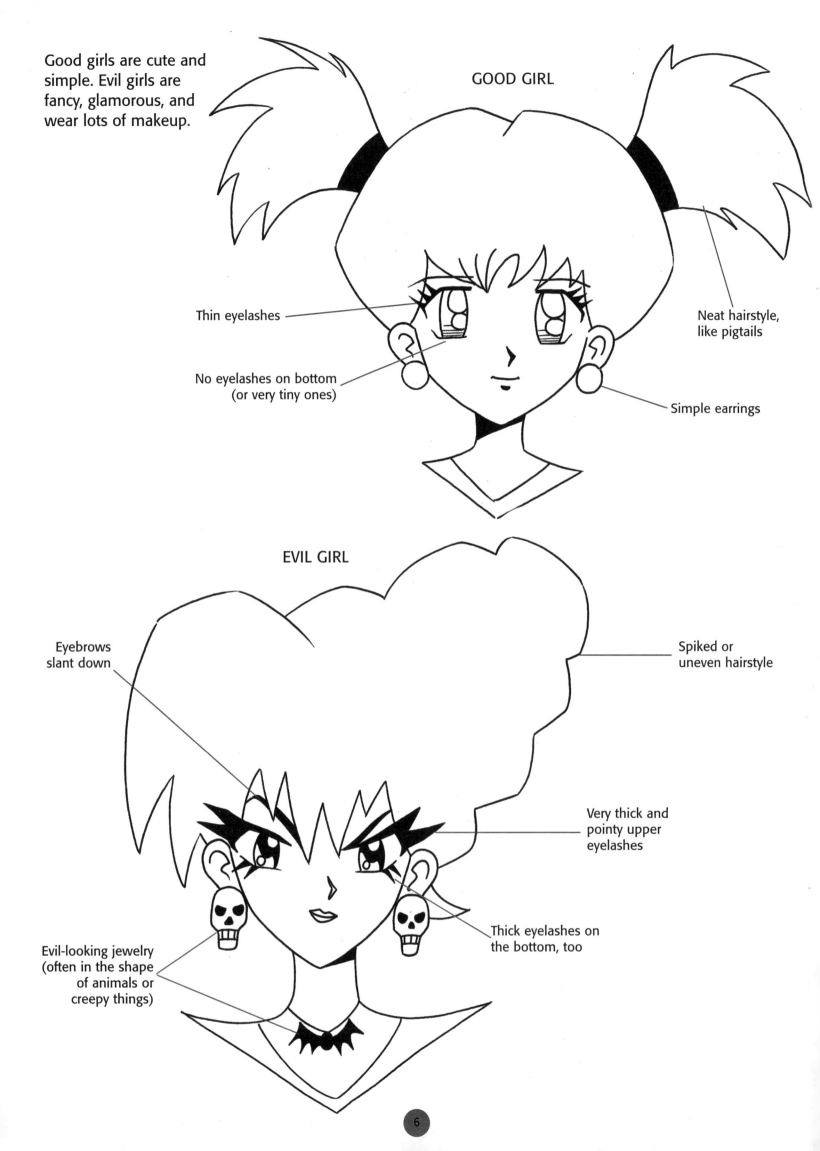

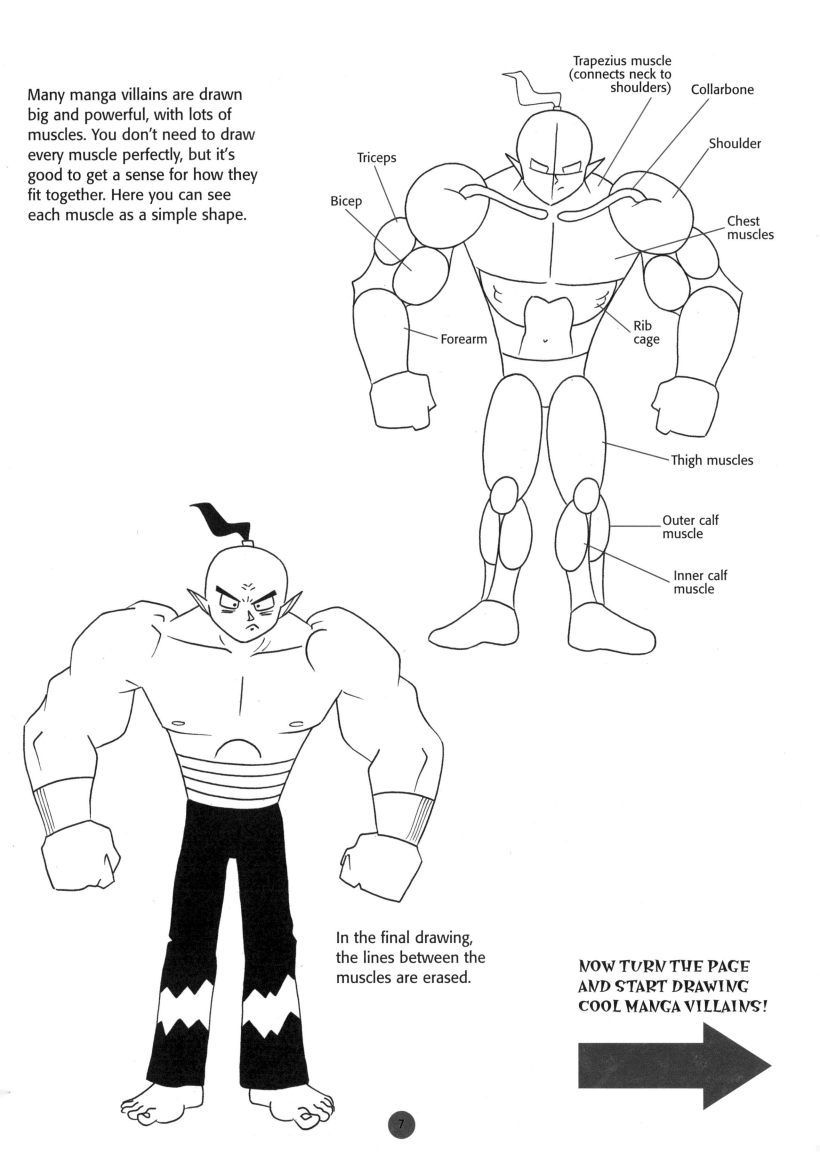

Many manga villains are drawn big and powerful, with lots of muscles. You don't need to draw every muscle perfectly, but it's good to get a sense for how they fit together. Here you can see each muscle as a simple shape.

Trapezius muscle (connects neck to shoulders)

Collarbone

Shoulder

Triceps

Bicep

Chest muscles

Forearm

Rib cage

Thigh muscles

Outer calf muscle

Inner calf muscle

In the final drawing, the lines between the muscles are erased.

NOW TURN THE PAGE AND START DRAWING COOL MANGA VILLAINS!

CRAZED KOOK

1

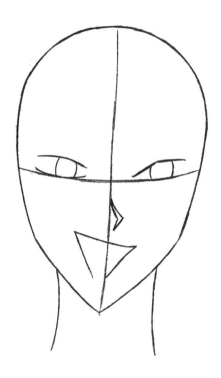

2

3

4

STREET FIGHTER

EVIL ELF

1

2

3

4

SHE-ALIEN

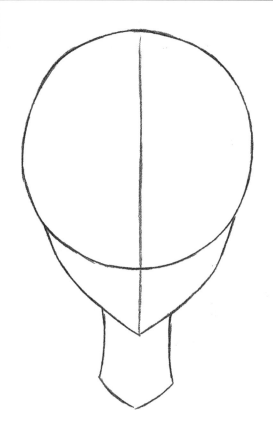

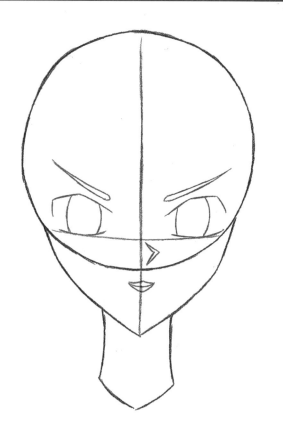

SWORD FIGHTER

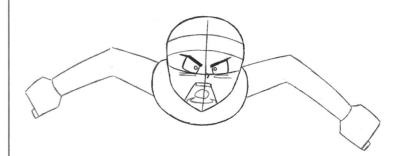

SKULL PRINCESS

SINISTER SMILE

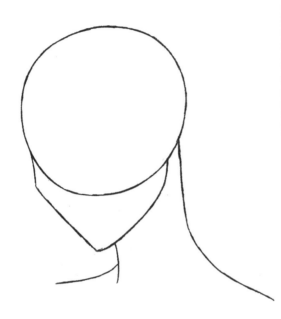

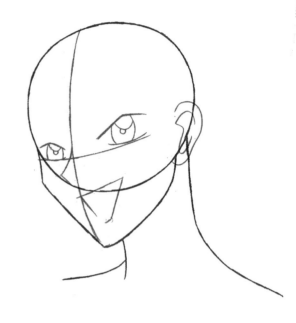

BATTLESHIP COMMANDER

1

2

3

4

EVIL BRAIN

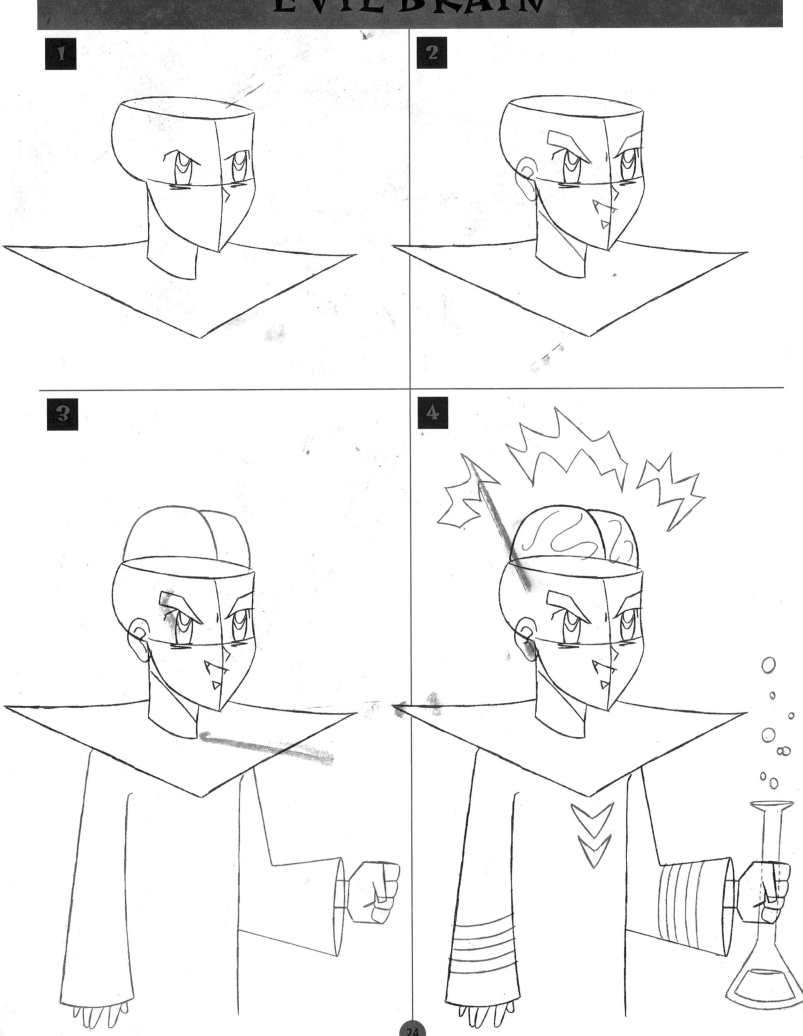

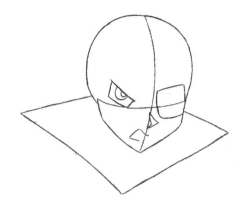

1

2

3

4

SPIKE FIST

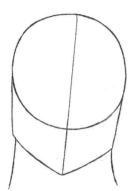

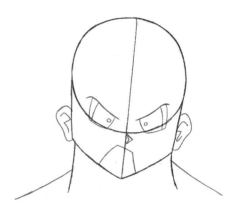

MAGIC WITCH

1

2

3

4

1

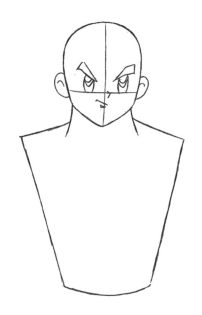

2

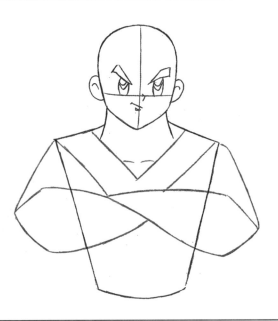

3

4

LOCKED-UP LUNKHEAD

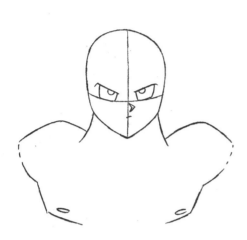

HALF-METAL MAN

1

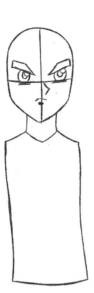

2

3

4

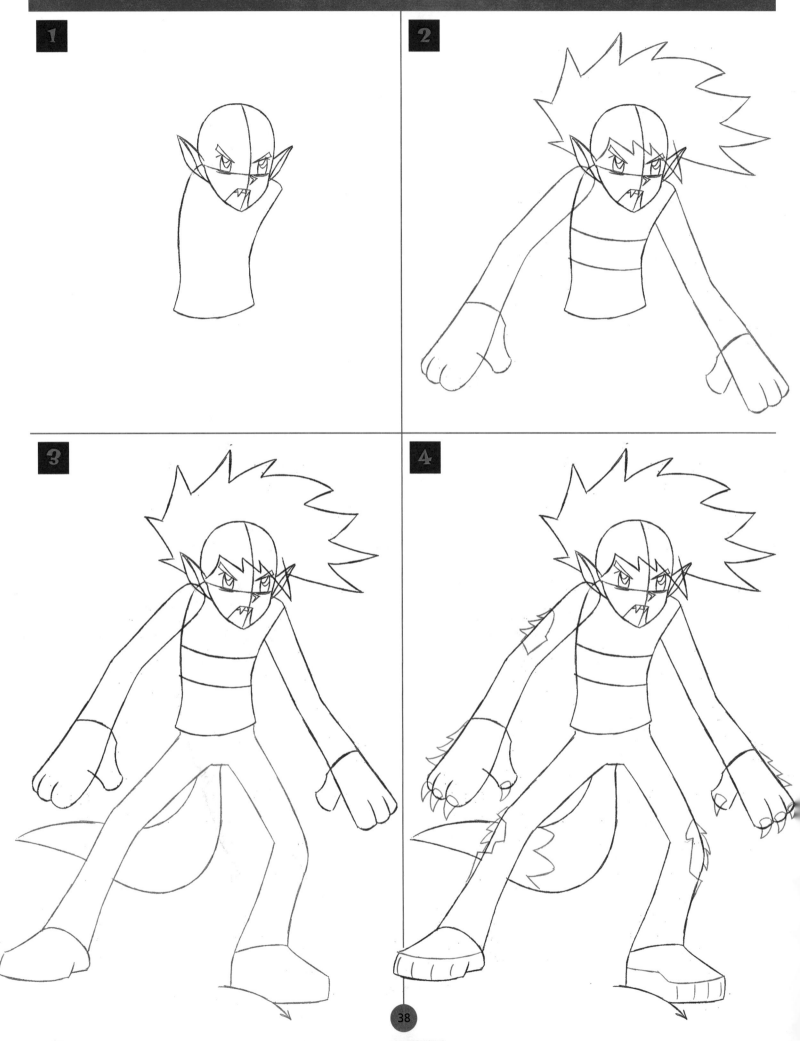

1

2

3

4

QUEEN VAMPREENA

1

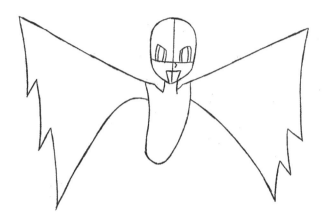

2

3

4

1

2

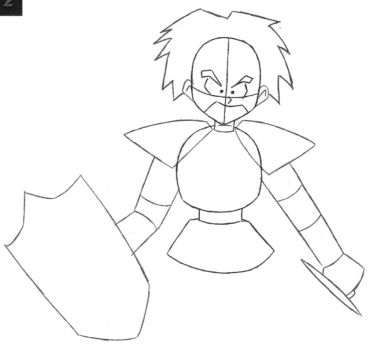

3

4

JEWEL KEEPER

1

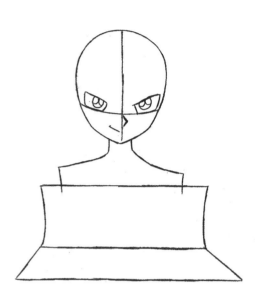

2

3

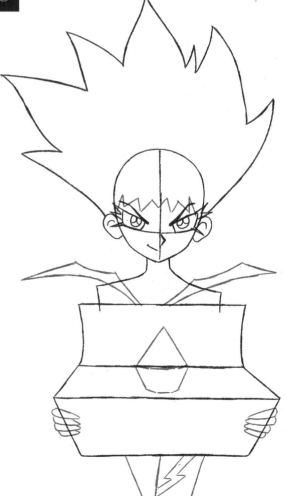

4

HORNED MUTANT

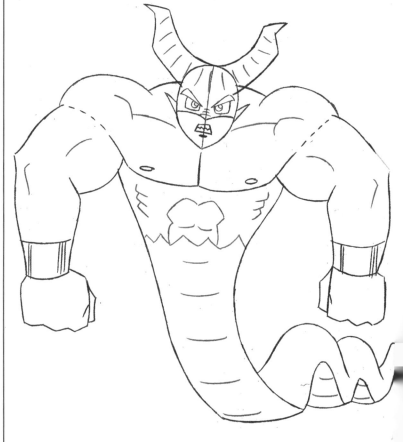

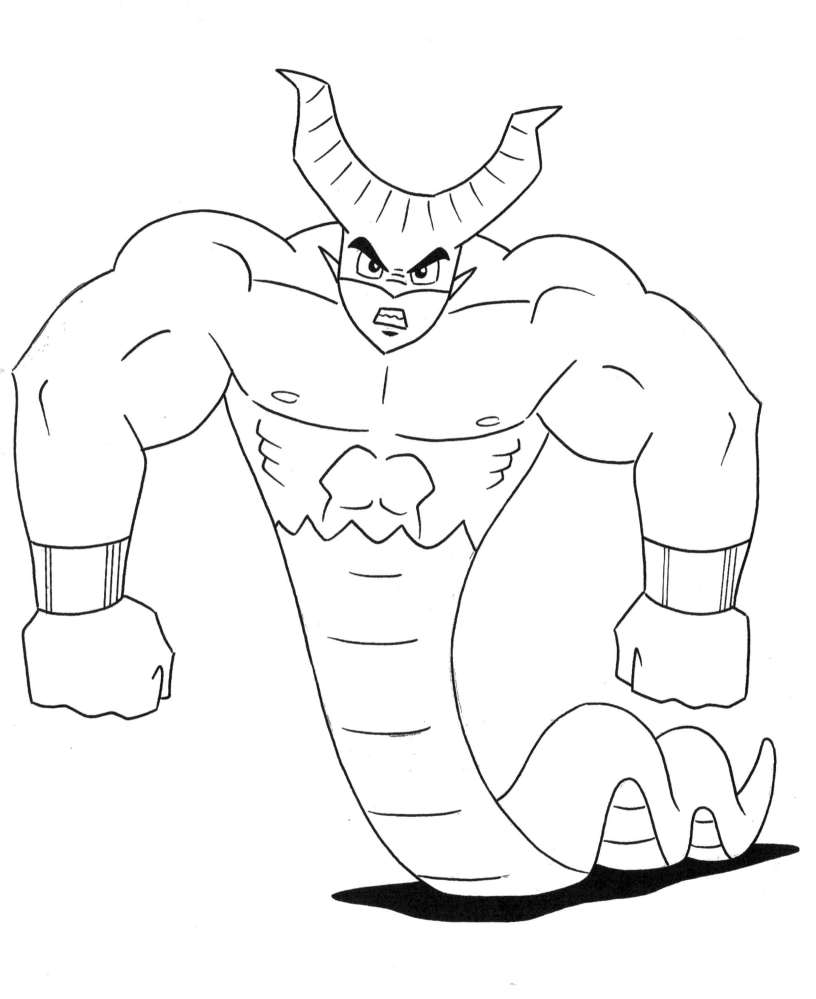

COLD CASH

KNIGHT ATTACK

1

2

3

4

CYBER SOLDIER

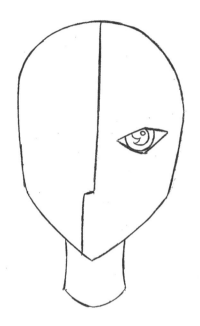

LIGHTNING FINGER

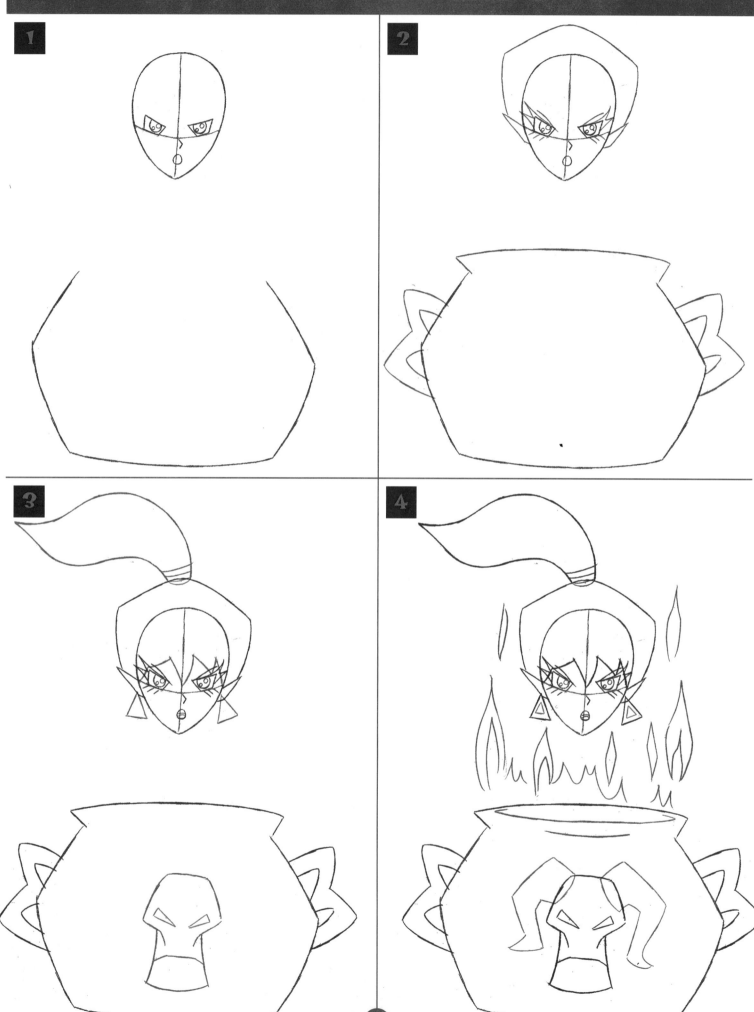

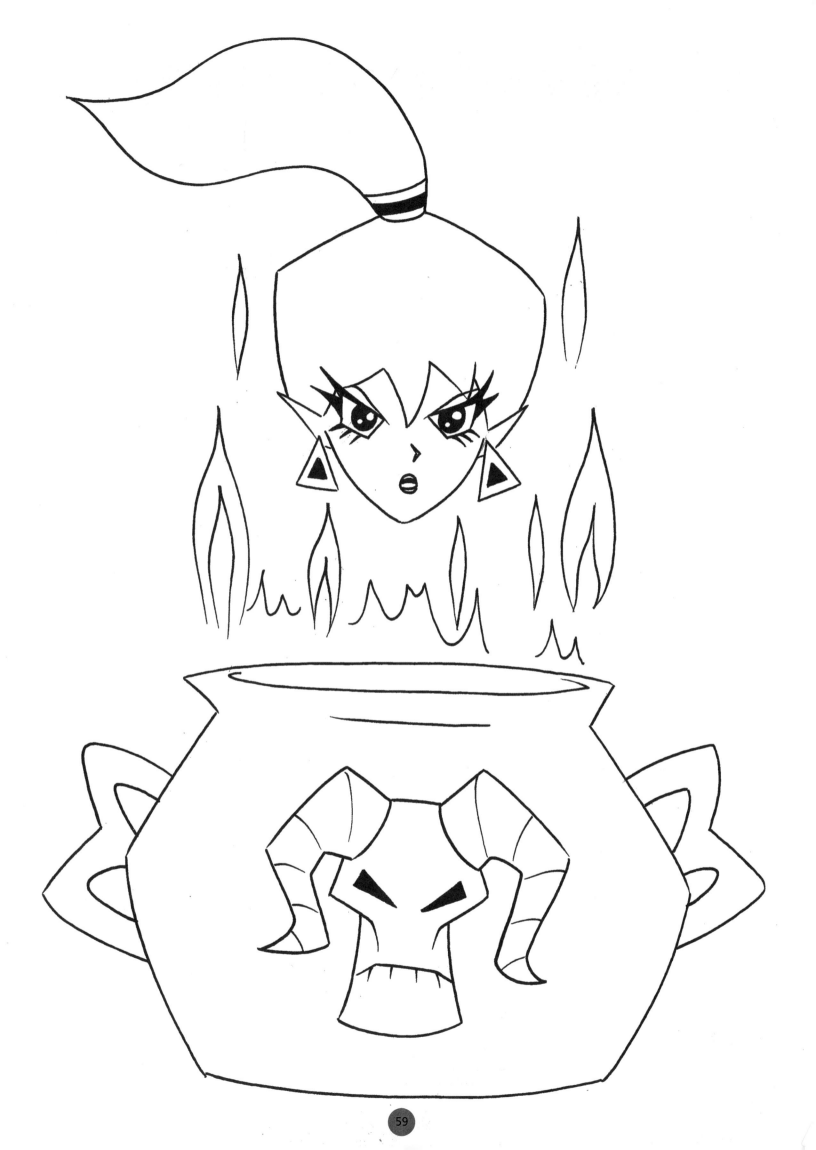

WICKED WARLOCK

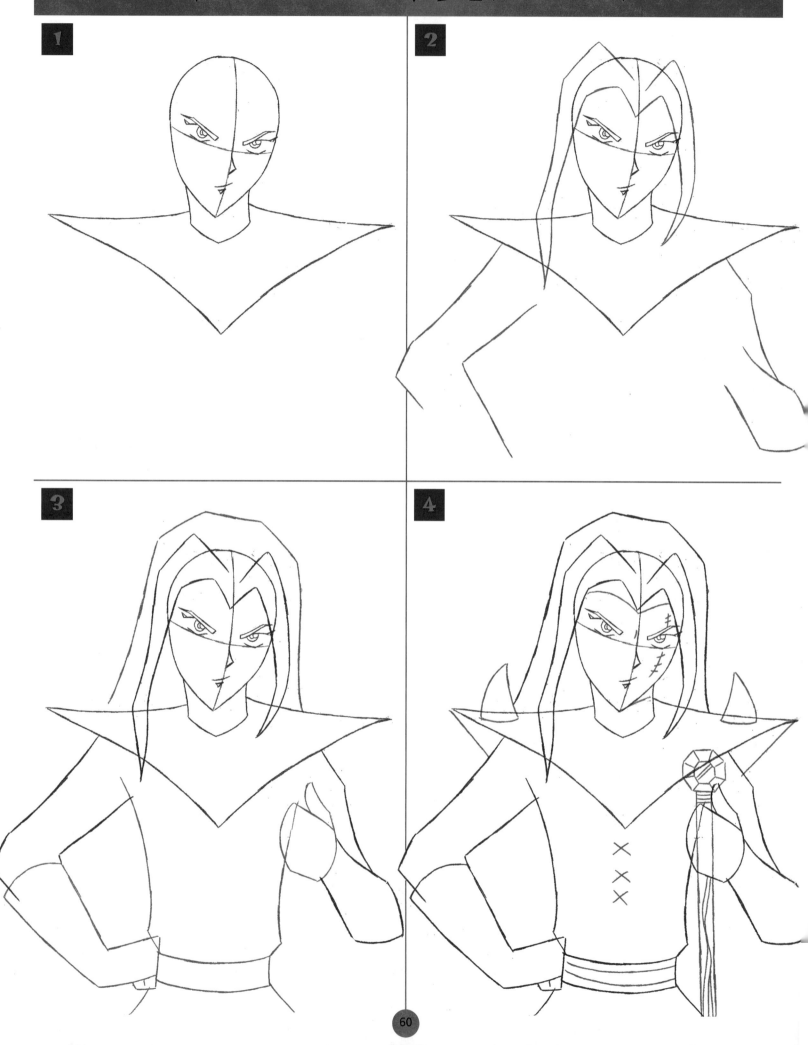

MONEYMAKER

Dedicated to Isabella, Francesca, and Maria

Senior Editor: Julie Mazur
Designer: Bob Fillie, Graphiti Design, Inc.
Production Manager: Hector Campbell
Text set in 13-pt Formata Regular

All drawings by Christopher Hart.

First published in 2004 by
Watson-Guptill Publications,
a division of VNU Business Media, Inc.
770 Broadway, New York, NY 10003
www.watsonguptill.com

Library of Congress Cataloging-in-Publication Data
Hart, Christopher.
Xtreme art : draw manga villains! / Christopher Hart.
p. cm. -- (Xtreme art)
ISBN 0-8230-0370-1
1. Comic books, strips, etc.--Japan--Technique--Juvenile literature.
2. Villains in art--Juvenile literature. I. Title: Extreme art. II. Title.
NC1764.5.J3H375 2004
741.5--dc22   2003019776

Printed in U. S. A.

First printing, 2004

1 2 3 4 5 6 7 8 / 11 10 09 08 07 06 05 04